Relaxation Gifts for Men with Anxiety

Thoughtful Ideas to Calm the Mind, Soothe the Soul, and Reclaim Serenity

by

Margaret Behler

Copyright

Relaxation Gifts for Men with Anxiety: Thoughtful Ideas to Calm the Mind, Soothe the Soul, and Reclaim Serenity

by

Margaret Behler

Disclaimer

The stuff in this book is just for sharing general info. Margaret Behler isn't a health or mental health expert, so don't take this as professional medical or psychological advice. If you're thinking about changing up your health routine or getting help for anxiety or other mental issues, it's smart to talk to a professional healthcare person first.

Margaret and the publisher aren't saying that everything mentioned in the book will work for sure. If you decide to follow any advice in here, you're doing it at your own risk. They can't be blamed if something goes wrong because you used or misused any ideas from this book.

Remember, by diving into this book, you're agreeing not to hold Margaret, the publisher, or anyone else involved responsible for any problems that might come up from using the info inside.

About the Author

Margaret Behler is a passionate advocate for mental wellness and self-care. As a mother of two, she's witnessed firsthand the impact of anxiety on loved ones and is dedicated to helping others find peace. With a warm and empathetic voice, Margaret shares her insights and expertise in *"Relaxation Gifts for Men with Anxiety: Thoughtful Ideas to Calm the Mind, Soothe the Soul, and Reclaim Serenity"* drawing from her own experiences and extensive research. When she's not writing or spending time with her family, you can find Margaret practicing yoga or exploring nature. Her goal is to inspire others to prioritize their well-being and cultivate a more compassionate, relaxed life

Table of Content

Introduction

The Power of Thoughtful Gifting for Men with Anxiety

"Sometimes, the most productive thing you can do is relax." – Mark Black

While the world is becoming more aware of mental health issues, there's still a unique and often overlooked challenge that men face. For generations, men have been encouraged to keep their emotions locked away, resulting in unspoken stress and anxiety that too often go untreated. But now, the conversation is shifting. More men are courageously seeking help and learning healthier ways to care for their mental well-being.

As awareness of men's mental health grows, so does the recognition of how impactful simple acts of kindness can be. A thoughtful gift, for instance, can go beyond being just an item. When chosen with care, especially with relaxation and wellness in mind, it can symbolize empathy, support, and understanding.

In *Relaxation Gifts for Men with Anxiety: Thoughtful Ideas to Calm the Mind, Soothe the Soul, and Reclaim Serenity,* we explore the transformative power of carefully curated gifts designed for men who struggle with anxiety. From mindfulness tools to tech-free relaxation aids, this guide offers compassionate and practical ideas for choosing gifts that truly make a difference.

Why Men's Mental Health Deserves More Attention

Although we're making strides in reducing the stigma surrounding men's mental health, the conversation is still evolving. Many men grow up with the misconception that asking for help is a sign of weakness, which makes it harder for them to cope with their struggles. Studies have shown that while men experience similar levels of stress and anxiety as women, they're less likely to seek professional help. This gap highlights the urgent need to create supportive spaces and services specifically designed for men's needs.

Normalizing rest and self-care is crucial to overcoming these barriers. Gifts that promote well-being don't just offer temporary comfort; they also encourage the recipient to incorporate self-care into their routine. Through thoughtful gifting, we can help men better manage their anxiety and embrace a more balanced approach to mental health.

Gifting as a Tool for Emotional Support

A gift is more than just a physical object—it's a way of showing you care. Thoughtfully chosen gifts that promote relaxation can be powerful tools for offering emotional support. These gifts can express concern, inspire calm, and strengthen connections.

A well-chosen present can have a profound impact on someone's emotional well-being. It can bring comfort and encourage self-care practices that last long after the gift is given. From wellness subscriptions to weighted blankets and mindfulness journals, gifts that prioritize mental and emotional well-being offer both immediate relief and lasting benefits.

In this book, I'll guide you through the world of relaxation gifts, helping you choose thoughtful items that alleviate stress and promote inner peace. Each chapter provides unique insights and practical tips on selecting gifts that truly matter. By focusing on empathy and action, you'll discover how meaningful gifting can enhance well-being and help the men in your life find balance and fulfillment.

Welcome to a world where gifts are more than just tokens—they're tools for support, relaxation, and serenity.

Chapter 1

The Science Behind Relaxation Gifts

"Research shows that even small acts of kindness, like giving a gift, can reduce anxiety and boost happiness for both the giver and receiver."

In a world where stress and anxiety are increasingly prevalent, understanding how simple gestures can make a profound difference is crucial. This chapter delves into the science behind relaxation gifts, exploring how they can be more than just tokens of appreciation—they can be powerful tools for improving mental health and well-being. I'll uncover how stress affects the male mind and body, the psychological impact of gifts, and the role of sensory experiences in relaxation. Additionally, I'll examine how gifts can serve as pathways to self-care and why personalized gifts have a unique, lasting impact.

How Stress Affects the Male Mind and Body

Understanding the Physical and Mental Impact of Chronic Stress

Prolonged stress sets off a series of physiological reactions, including elevated cortisol levels, which can result in several health complications, including immune system weakness, digestive disorders, and hypertension. Stress has a comparable impact on mental health, exacerbating symptoms of anxiety and despair.

Prolonged stress damages the brain's ability to process information and control emotions, which makes people less productive, agitated, and hard to focus. Relationships both personally and professionally may suffer as a result, adding to the stress.

Men and women experience stress in different ways, with men frequently internalizing their emotions instead of seeking support. This suppression can make stress-related problems worse and make it more difficult to use healthy coping mechanisms.

How Relaxation Aids Recovery and Prevents Burnout

Engaging in relaxation techniques, such as deep breathing, meditation, and progressive muscle relaxation, helps reduce cortisol levels and promotes the activation of the parasympathetic nervous system, which counteracts the stress response.

Frequent relaxation techniques can increase resilience overall, enhancing one's capacity to manage stress and lowering the likelihood of burnout.

These routines promote emotional stability and mental clarity, which enhance quality of life. Relaxation can help maintain a better balance between work and personal life by preventing stress and its negative effects from building up.

Why Men Often Ignore or Suppress Their Stress Symptoms
Social norms and cultural expectations often discourage men from expressing vulnerability or seeking help, leading to a tendency to downplay or ignore stress symptoms.

This suppression may result in an accumulation of unresolved stress, which may show up as behavioral changes like irritability or withdrawal or as physical symptoms like headaches or gastrointestinal problems.

It is imperative to tackle cultural obstacles and foster candid conversations on mental health to motivate men to get suitable assistance and embrace efficacious techniques for managing stress.

The Psychological Power of Gifts

How Receiving Gifts Triggers Positive Emotions
Giving or receiving a gift can activate the reward centers of the brain, releasing endorphins and dopamine that lead to positive emotions.

Thoughtful and meaningful gifts have a greater emotional impact and strengthen the bond and feelings of gratitude between the giver and the recipient.

Receiving a present can make you feel happy and relieve tension temporarily. It also improves your mood and sense of wellbeing.

The Role of Surprise and Appreciation in Stress Reduction
Anxiety and tension can be balanced by the delight and excitement that surprises can arouse. A thoughtful gift's unpredictable nature adds a touch of surprise and joy.

Giving gifts as a way of showing gratitude can improve sentiments of social support and social relationships, both of which are important for stress management.

Receiving a gift that shows empathy and understanding can reaffirm the recipient's worth and promote their mental health.

Why Meaningful Gifts Can Encourage Long-Term Relaxation Habits

Gifts that promote relaxation can serve as reminders to prioritize self-care, helping individuals incorporate relaxation practices into their daily routines.

Meaningful gifts, such as mindfulness journals or aromatherapy kits, provide tools for managing stress and encourage the development of healthy relaxation habits.

By offering gifts that support ongoing well-being, givers can contribute to the recipient's long-term mental health and stress management strategies.

How Sensory Experiences Impact Relaxation

The Effects of Touch, Smell, and Sound on Anxiety

Sensory experiences play a significant role in relaxation, with touch, smell, and sound influencing the body's stress response. Gentle touch and comforting textures can induce a calming effect, while soothing sounds and pleasant scents can enhance relaxation.

The brain's response to sensory stimuli can either exacerbate or alleviate stress, making it important to choose sensory-rich gifts that promote calmness and tranquility.

Understanding the individual's sensory preferences can help in selecting gifts that provide the most effective relaxation benefits.

The Calming Impact of Sensory-Rich Gifts (e.g., Aromatherapy, Weighted Blankets)

Aromatherapy products, such as essential oils and diffusers, can influence mood and stress levels through the olfactory system, providing a soothing effect and promoting relaxation.

Weighted blankets offer deep touch pressure, which can enhance feelings of security and calm, reducing anxiety and improving sleep quality.

Sensory-rich gifts like these can provide immediate and lasting relief, enhancing the overall relaxation experience.

How Specific Senses Can Trigger Immediate Relaxation

Certain scents, such as lavender or chamomile, have been shown to have calming effects on the nervous system, reducing anxiety and promoting relaxation.

Soft textures and comforting materials, such as plush blankets or cozy socks, can provide physical comfort and enhance feelings of relaxation.

Calming sounds, such as nature sounds or gentle music, can create a serene environment, helping to alleviate stress and promote mental well-being.

Gifts as a Pathway to Self-Care

How Gifts Can Introduce or Reinforce Self-Care Routines

Gifts that promote self-care can help individuals establish or strengthen relaxation routines, encouraging regular practice and integrating self-care into daily life.

Examples include mindfulness journals that facilitate reflection and meditation, or fitness equipment that supports physical well-being and stress management.

By providing tools that encourage self-care, gifts can empower individuals to take an active role in managing their mental health and well-being.

Examples of Gifts that Promote Daily Mindfulness
Mindfulness journals with guided prompts can help individuals develop a consistent mindfulness practice, fostering emotional resilience and reducing stress.

Meditation cushions and mats can enhance comfort during mindfulness and meditation sessions, making it easier to incorporate these practices into daily routines.

Subscriptions to mindfulness apps or online classes can provide ongoing support and resources for developing and maintaining mindfulness practices.

Building Self-Care into Everyday Life Through Gift-Giving
Gifts that encourage self-care can serve as reminders to prioritize relaxation and well-being, integrating these practices into everyday life.

Personalized gifts, such as custom wellness kits or tailored relaxation tools, can reinforce the importance of self-care and make it easier to maintain healthy habits.

By selecting gifts that align with the recipient's interests and needs, givers can support the development of sustainable self-care routines.

Why Personalized Gifts Matter More

The Psychological Benefits of Receiving a Tailored Gift

Personalized gifts show that the giver has put thought and effort into selecting something that resonates with the recipient's unique preferences and needs.

Tailored gifts can enhance feelings of validation and appreciation, reinforcing the recipient's sense of worth and connection.

The psychological impact of receiving a personalized gift can contribute to improved emotional well-being and stress management.

How Personalization Shows Thoughtfulness and Care

Personalizing gifts demonstrates a deep level of consideration and understanding, which can strengthen relationships and build trust.

Thoughtful personalization reflects the giver's empathy and commitment to addressing the recipient's specific needs and preferences.

Personalization can also enhance the practical value of the gift, ensuring that it is relevant and useful for the recipient's relaxation and well-being.

Examples of Personalized Relaxation Gifts for Men with Anxiety

Custom engraved relaxation tools, such as stress balls or massage rollers, can provide a unique and practical touch.

Monogrammed journals or mindfulness planners can offer a personal connection to daily self-care practices.

Personalized aromatherapy kits, featuring the recipient's favorite scents, can create a customized relaxation experience tailored to their preferences.

Chapter 2

Mindfulness and Meditation Gifts

"Meditation is not a way of making your mind quiet. It's a way of entering the quiet that is already there." – Deepak Chopra

Understanding the Science Behind Relaxation Gifts: How Simple Gestures Make a Big Impact

In today's fast-paced world, where stress and anxiety seem to be constant companions, it's essential to recognize how small gestures can profoundly impact someone's well-being. This chapter uncovers the science behind relaxation gifts, demonstrating how these tokens of appreciation can go beyond their material value to become powerful tools for improving mental health. I'll explore how stress affects the male mind and body, delve into the psychological effects of gifting, and examine the calming power of sensory experiences. I'll also highlight how thoughtful gifts can serve as a gateway to self-care and why personalization gives them lasting meaning.

The Impact of Stress on the Male Mind and Body

Understanding Chronic Stress: Physical and Mental Consequences

When stress becomes a regular part of life, it triggers a chain reaction in the body—most notably, an increase in cortisol levels. Over time, this can lead to a host of health issues, including a weakened immune system, digestive problems, and high blood pressure. But stress isn't just a physical burden; it takes a heavy toll on mental health too, contributing to heightened anxiety and depression.

Prolonged stress can impair the brain's ability to process information and regulate emotions, leaving people feeling overwhelmed, irritable, and unable to focus. This mental strain can spill over into personal and professional relationships, adding yet another layer of stress to an already challenging situation.

Men often handle stress differently than women, tending to internalize their emotions rather than seek support. This tendency to bottle things up can worsen stress-related issues and make it harder to adopt healthy coping mechanisms.

Relaxation as a Path to Recovery and Resilience

Relaxation techniques like deep breathing, meditation, and progressive muscle relaxation help to lower cortisol levels and activate the parasympathetic nervous system, which counters the body's stress response. By regularly practicing these techniques, individuals can build greater resilience, enhancing their ability to manage stress and reducing the risk of burnout.

These relaxation practices promote emotional stability and mental clarity, leading to an improved quality of life. By preventing stress from building up, they also help individuals strike a healthier balance between work and personal life.

Why Men Often Suppress Stress Symptoms

Societal norms and cultural expectations have long discouraged men from showing vulnerability or seeking help, leading many to downplay or ignore their stress symptoms. This suppression often results in unresolved stress, which can manifest as irritability, withdrawal, or even physical symptoms like headaches and digestive issues.

Breaking down these cultural barriers is essential to encouraging open discussions about mental health. By fostering an environment where men feel safe to express their struggles, we can help them find the support they need and adopt effective stress-management techniques.

The Psychological Power of Gifts

How Gifts Trigger Positive Emotions

Receiving a gift, especially one that's thoughtful and meaningful, activates the brain's reward centers, releasing feel-good chemicals like endorphins and dopamine. This surge of positive emotions strengthens the bond between giver and recipient and fosters feelings of gratitude.

A well-chosen gift can instantly lift someone's mood, temporarily easing their stress and contributing to a greater sense of well-being.

The Role of Surprise and Appreciation in Reducing Stress

Surprises bring a sense of joy and excitement that can counterbalance anxiety and stress. The unexpected nature of a thoughtful gift adds an element of delight that can momentarily distract from life's pressures.

Gifts given as tokens of appreciation also enhance feelings of social support, which is crucial for managing stress. When someone receives a gift that shows empathy and understanding, it reinforces their sense of worth and can have a lasting positive impact on their mental health.

How Meaningful Gifts Encourage Long-Term Relaxation Habits
Gifts that promote relaxation can serve as gentle reminders to prioritize self-care, helping recipients integrate relaxation into their daily routines. Whether it's a mindfulness journal or an aromatherapy kit, these gifts provide the tools to manage stress and develop healthy relaxation habits.

By offering gifts that support well-being, you're not just giving a momentary reprieve—you're contributing to the recipient's long-term mental health and resilience.

The Role of Sensory Experiences in Relaxation

The Influence of Touch, Smell, and Sound on Anxiety
Sensory experiences are powerful when it comes to relaxation. The soothing feel of soft textures, the calming sound of gentle music, and the comforting scent of essential oils all play a role in reducing stress. These sensory inputs can either heighten or alleviate stress, making it important to choose gifts that promote a calming atmosphere.

By understanding someone's sensory preferences, you can select gifts that are most likely to bring them peace and relaxation.

Sensory-Rich Gifts for Calming Effects (e.g., Aromatherapy, Weighted Blankets)
Aromatherapy products, such as essential oils and diffusers, tap into the power of scent to influence mood and reduce stress levels. Weighted blankets offer deep touch pressure, which can provide a sense of security, calm anxiety, and even improve sleep quality.

Gifts that engage the senses offer both immediate relief and lasting relaxation, making them ideal for anyone seeking peace of mind.

How Specific Senses Can Trigger Immediate Relaxation
Certain scents, like lavender or chamomile, are known for their calming effects on the nervous system, helping to ease anxiety and promote relaxation. Soft, comforting materials—whether it's a plush blanket or cozy socks—provide physical comfort that enhances the relaxation experience. And soothing sounds, from nature recordings to gentle music, can create a peaceful environment that promotes mental well-being.

Gifts as Pathways to Self-Care

Introducing or Reinforcing Self-Care Through Gifts
Gifts that encourage self-care can help individuals establish or strengthen relaxation routines, making it easier to incorporate these practices into their daily lives. For example, mindfulness journals with guided prompts can foster reflection and meditation, while fitness equipment can support physical well-being and stress management.

By giving gifts that promote self-care, you're empowering individuals to take an active role in maintaining their mental health and overall well-being.

Examples of Gifts that Promote Daily Mindfulness
Mindfulness journals with thoughtful prompts can help individuals cultivate a consistent mindfulness practice, reducing stress and building emotional resilience. Meditation cushions and mats enhance comfort during mindfulness sessions, making it easier to maintain a regular practice. Subscriptions to mindfulness apps or online classes can provide ongoing support, helping recipients develop and sustain mindfulness habits.

Building Self-Care into Everyday Life Through Gift-Giving

Gifts that encourage self-care act as daily reminders to prioritize relaxation and well-being. Personalized gifts, such as custom wellness kits or tailored relaxation tools, make it easier to maintain healthy habits and integrate self-care into everyday routines. By selecting gifts that align with the recipient's unique needs and interests, you can support their journey toward lasting relaxation and mental balance.

Why Personalized Gifts Matter More

The Psychological Benefits of Receiving a Tailored Gift

A personalized gift shows that you've put thought and effort into selecting something that resonates with the recipient's specific preferences and needs. This kind of gift can boost feelings of validation and appreciation, reinforcing the recipient's sense of worth and connection.

Receiving a tailored gift can also improve emotional well-being, making it a powerful tool for stress management.

How Personalization Reflects Thoughtfulness and Care

Personalizing a gift demonstrates a deep level of consideration and empathy, which can strengthen relationships and build trust. It shows that you've taken the time to understand the recipient's individual needs, making the gift more meaningful and impactful.

Personalization also enhances the practical value of the gift, ensuring that it's not only thoughtful but also relevant and useful to the recipient's relaxation and well-being.

Examples of Personalized Relaxation Gifts for Men with Anxiety

Consider gifts like custom-engraved relaxation tools—such as stress balls or massage rollers—that combine practicality with a personal touch. Monogrammed journals or mindfulness planners add a personalized connection to daily self-care practices. Or, create a customized aromatherapy kit with the recipient's favorite scents, tailored to their preferences for a truly unique relaxation experience.

Chapter 3

Tech-Free Relaxation Gifts

"Disconnect to Reconnect"

Finding genuine relaxation can be difficult in a world surrounded by screens and digital notifications. Embracing tech-free relaxation presents provides a nice respite from the digital bustle and promotes genuine moments of calm. This chapter explores the importance of detaching from technology through thoughtful presents that encourage relaxation and inner serenity.

The Necessity of a Digital Detox

How Constant Connectivity Increases Stress and Anxiety

Information Overload: The constant barrage of news updates, social media notifications, and work-related messages can overwhelm the mind, heightening stress and anxiety. The relentless need to stay connected creates urgency and contributes to mental exhaustion.

Sleep Disruption: Exposure to screens, particularly before bedtime, disrupts sleep patterns due to blue light, which further exacerbates stress and anxiety, creating a continuous cycle of unrest.

Social Comparison: Social media often showcases idealized versions of life, leading to feelings of inadequacy as users compare themselves to others, increasing stress and anxiety.

The Benefits of Taking a Break from Screens

Enhanced Focus: Regular breaks from screens help clear mental clutter, leading to improved focus and emotional well-being. This mental clarity fosters relaxation and a more balanced state of mind.

Better Sleep: Reducing screen time, especially before sleep, improves sleep quality by reducing disruptions caused by blue light, supporting overall mental health and reducing anxiety.

Increased Presence: Disconnecting from digital distractions promotes mindfulness and enables more meaningful engagement with the present moment and with others.

Gift Ideas that Encourage Unplugging

Creating Tech-Free Zones

Digital Detox Spaces: Gifts that help create environments for digital detox, such as cozy reading nooks or relaxation corners, encourage individuals to step away from screens and engage in calming activities.

Offline Activities

Analog Hobbies: Consider gifts that promote offline hobbies, such as physical books, journaling supplies, or creative tools, offering a satisfying alternative to screen time.

Books and Journals: Analog Relaxation Tools

The Relaxing Power of Reading

Escape and Immersion: Reading offers a mental escape from daily stressors, immersing the mind in different worlds and fostering relaxation. A good book provides a form of mental rest and rejuvenation.

Mindfulness Through Books: Titles focusing on mindfulness, self-care, and personal growth guide readers towards relaxation and healthier coping strategies.

Reduced Screen Time: Opting for physical books over digital formats minimizes screen exposure, creating a more serene reading experience.

Book Recommendations for Mindfulness and Well-Being

Self-Help and Wellness: Books on mindfulness and stress management, such as *"The Art of Happiness"* by *Dalai Lama* or *"The Power of Now"* by *Eckhart Tolle*, offer practical techniques for reducing anxiety and finding inner peace.

Fiction for Escape: Uplifting novels, like *"The Alchemist"* by *Paulo Coelho* or *"A Man Called Ove"* by *Fredrik Backman*, provide comforting escapes from daily stressors.

Inspirational Biographies: Biographies of individuals who have overcome challenges or embraced mindfulness, such as *"Becoming"* by *Michelle Obama*, offer both insight and motivation.

Journals for Reflection and Unplugging

Reflective Prompts: Guided journals for reflection, gratitude, and mindfulness encourage offline exploration of thoughts and feelings, fostering introspection and stress relief.

Daily Logs: Journals that track mood, stress levels, and achievements offer a structured approach to managing anxiety and celebrating progress.

Creative Expression: Journals with space for creative writing, doodling, or personal projects provide relaxation and self-expression free from digital distractions.

Nature-Inspired Gifts

The Calming Impact of Nature

Natural Serenity: Exposure to nature is known to reduce stress and promote relaxation. Natural environments provide a calming effect and help lower anxiety levels.

Biophilia: The concept of biophilia highlights our innate connection to nature. Integrating natural elements into daily life can enhance well-being and offer a soothing escape from urban stressors.

Mindfulness in Nature: Spending time in natural settings encourages mindfulness and helps individuals reconnect with their surroundings, fostering a sense of peace.

Gifts Bringing Nature Indoors

Indoor Plants: Houseplants improve air quality and add natural beauty to indoor spaces. Easy-care options like snake plants, peace lilies, and succulents create a calming environment.

Nature Sound Machines: Devices that play soothing nature sounds—such as rain, ocean waves, or birdsong—create a peaceful ambiance and aid relaxation, masking background noise and promoting tranquility.

Nature-Inspired Décor: Gifts like nature-themed artwork, botanical prints, or natural textures in home décor bring a calming, nature-inspired atmosphere into living spaces.

Creative Hobbies for Stress Relief

How Creative Activities Alleviate Stress

Expressive Outlets: Creative activities provide constructive outlets for emotions and self-expression. Engaging in art, crafts, or hands-on projects can be therapeutic and reduce stress.

Mindful Engagement: Creating something new fosters mindfulness and focus, helping individuals stay present and alleviate anxiety. It offers a sense of accomplishment and satisfaction.

Active Relaxation: Creative hobbies serve as active relaxation methods, offering a break from daily stressors and promoting mental well-being through productive engagement.

Gifts that Foster Creative Expression and Relaxation

Art Supplies: High-quality art supplies, such as sketchbooks, paints, or drawing tools, inspire creativity and offer stress relief. Consider sets catering to various interests and skill levels.

Craft Kits: Pre-packaged craft kits for model-building or DIY home décor projects offer structured ways to explore creativity and relaxation.

Workshops or Classes: Access to art workshops or creative classes provides opportunities for learning and personal growth, fostering relaxation through creative pursuits.

Why Creativity is a Powerful Tool for Managing Anxiety

Emotional Release Through Creativity

Constructive Expression: Creative activities allow individuals to process and release emotions constructively, contributing to reduced anxiety and improved mental health.

Flow State: Creative pursuits often lead to a state of flow, where individuals are fully immersed and focused. This state offers a temporary escape from stress and anxiety.

Skill Development: Developing new skills through creative activities boosts self-esteem and confidence, supporting overall well-being and resilience against anxiety.

Board Games and Puzzles for Relaxation

How Analog Games Reduce Stress

Social Interaction: Playing board games and puzzles often involves social interaction, providing a sense of connection and support. This can help alleviate feelings of isolation and stress.

Mindfulness Through Play: Games and puzzles require concentration and problem-solving, serving as a form of mindfulness and distraction from anxious thoughts.

Relaxation and Enjoyment: The enjoyable nature of games and puzzles offers a break from daily stressors, contributing to relaxation and well-being.

Gift Ideas: Calming Puzzles, Strategy Games, or Solo Challenges

Calming Puzzles: Gift jigsaw puzzles featuring serene landscapes or soothing designs to promote relaxation through focused, meditative activity.

Strategy Board Games: Games that involve strategic thinking and problem-solving, such as chess or Settlers of Catan, offer a mentally engaging and stress-relieving experience.

Solo Challenges: Gifts like brainteasers, Sudoku books, or logic puzzles provide solo relaxation and mental stimulation without digital distractions.

The Benefits of Tech-Free Fun

Stress Reduction Through Engaging Activities

Mental Break: Fun, tech-free activities offer a mental break from digital overload, reducing stress through enjoyable and immersive experiences.

Cognitive Engagement: Focusing on games and puzzles enhances cognitive function and problem-solving skills, contributing to relaxation and mental well-being.

Mindful Play: Playing games and solving puzzles encourages mindfulness and helps shift focus away from stressors, promoting a sense of calm and enjoyment.

Chapter 4

Aromatherapy and Scent-Based Relaxation Gifts

"Scents can evoke powerful emotional reactions, making them a perfect tool for relaxation."

Aromatherapy harnesses the power of scents to foster relaxation, reduce stress, and promote overall well-being. The right fragrances can trigger emotional responses and create calming environments that help soothe anxiety. This chapter delves into various scent-based relaxation gifts and how they can be utilized to enhance mental peace and relaxation.

Essential Oils for Anxiety Relief

The Science Behind Aromatherapy for Stress Reduction

Olfactory System and Emotions: The sense of smell is directly linked to the limbic system, the part of the brain responsible for emotions and memory. Aromatherapy uses essential oils to influence this system and evoke calming responses.

Impact on Stress Hormones: Certain essential oils have been shown to reduce levels of cortisol, the stress hormone, and promote relaxation. Research indicates that inhaling these oils can decrease anxiety and improve mood.

Supporting Evidence: Studies and clinical trials have demonstrated the efficacy of aromatherapy in managing stress and anxiety, highlighting its benefits as a complementary approach to traditional therapies.

Top Essential Oils for Calming Anxiety

Lavender: Known for its soothing properties, lavender essential oil is often used to alleviate anxiety, improve sleep, and create a calming environment. It is a versatile oil that can be used in various forms, including diffusers and topical applications.

Chamomile: Chamomile oil is renowned for its relaxing effects and can help reduce symptoms of anxiety and promote restful sleep. It's often used in combination with other calming oils.

Frankincense: This oil is valued for its grounding properties and ability to promote a sense of inner peace and calm. It can be particularly useful in meditation practices and stress management.

Gifting Essential Oil Kits, Diffusers, or Roll-Ons

Essential Oil Kits: Pre-packaged kits that include a selection of essential oils provide a comprehensive approach to aromatherapy. Look for kits that include popular calming oils and instructions for use.

Diffusers: Essential oil diffusers disperse scents into the air, creating a relaxing atmosphere. Consider gifting ultrasonic diffusers, which use water to diffuse oils and add humidity to the air.

Roll-Ons: Roll-on bottles filled with diluted essential oils are convenient for on-the-go relaxation. They can be applied directly to pulse points for immediate stress relief.

Scented Candles and Relaxation

How Specific Scents Help Create a Calming Environment

Lavender and Vanilla: Scents like lavender and vanilla are well-known for their relaxing properties. Lavender helps to calm the mind, while vanilla adds a soothing, comforting aroma.

Citrus and Eucalyptus: Citrus scents like orange and lemon can uplift the mood and energize, while eucalyptus offers a refreshing, clean scent that helps with mental clarity and relaxation.

Sandalwood and Cedarwood: These earthy scents provide grounding effects and help create a tranquil environment. They are ideal for creating a peaceful setting for meditation or relaxation.

Candle Recommendations for Stress Relief

Soy and Beeswax Candles: Choose candles made from natural materials like soy or beeswax, which burn cleaner and release fewer toxins into the air. Look for candles with essential oils for added relaxation benefits.

Scent Combinations: Go for candles that feature calming blends, such as lavender-chamomile or sandalwood-vanilla. These combinations enhance relaxation and create a soothing atmosphere.

Quality Brands: Consider high-quality candle brands known for their long-lasting scents and clean burning. Brands like Yankee Candle, Bath & Body Works, or local artisans can offer great options.

Pairing Candles with Other Gifts for a Relaxing Atmosphere

Gift Sets: Combine scented candles with other relaxation gifts, such as bath salts or essential oil diffusers, to create a complete relaxation package. This combination enhances the overall experience and provides multiple avenues for stress relief.

Relaxation Kits: Create personalized relaxation kits that include candles, soothing teas, and cozy blankets to promote a restful environment. These kits can be tailored to the recipient's preferences for a thoughtful touch.

Ambiance Enhancers: Pair candles with other elements like soft music or calming visuals (e.g., nature scenes) to create a holistic relaxation experience.

Natural Scent-Based Products

Lotions, Bath Salts, and Balms Infused with Calming Scents

Lotions and Creams: Lotions with essential oils such as lavender, chamomile, or sandalwood provide both moisturizing benefits and aromatherapy. They can be applied to the skin for a relaxing sensory experience.

Bath Salts: Bath salts infused with calming scents help enhance the bath experience by promoting relaxation and relieving muscle tension. Epsom salts combined with essential oils create a spa-like experience at home.

Balms and Soothing Rubs: Balms and rubs containing essential oils can be used for targeted relief of stress and tension. These products are ideal for applying to sore muscles or pulse points.

How These Products Can Create a Spa-Like Relaxation Experience at Home

Home Spa Kits: Create home spa experiences by combining products like bath salts, lotions, and essential oil-infused candles. This setup allows for a luxurious and relaxing experience without leaving home.

Routine Integration: Incorporate these products into daily or weekly self-care routines to promote consistent relaxation and stress relief. Encourage recipients to use them regularly for ongoing benefits.

Sensory Appeal: Choose products with complementary scents and textures to enhance the sensory experience. The combination of soothing scents and tactile experiences contributes to a greater sense of relaxation.

Gift Bundles that Combine Multiple Scent-Based Products

Custom Bundles: Create custom gift bundles that include a selection of natural scent-based products. For example, pair bath salts with matching lotions and essential oils for a cohesive relaxation package.

Themed Sets: Develop themed bundles based on relaxation goals, such as sleep aids or stress relief. Each set can include items like calming bath products, soothing balms, and aromatherapy essentials.

Subscription Options: Consider gifting subscription boxes that deliver natural scent-based products on a regular basis. This option provides ongoing relaxation and self-care opportunities.

Customizing Scent-Based Gifts

How to Choose Scents Based on the Recipient's Preferences

Personal Preferences: Take note of the recipient's favorite scents or any known sensitivities to certain aromas. This ensures that the gift is tailored to their individual tastes and needs.

Mood and Purpose: Choose scents based on the desired effect, such as calming lavender for relaxation or invigorating citrus for energy. Aligning scents with the recipient's goals enhances the effectiveness of the gift.

Allergies and Sensitivities: Be mindful of any allergies or sensitivities the recipient may have. Opt for hypoallergenic or natural products to avoid adverse reactions.

Personalizing Gift Sets with Their Favorite Calming Scents
Customized Kits: Create personalized gift sets that include the recipient's favorite scents in various forms, such as candles, essential oils, and lotions. This personal touch demonstrates thoughtfulness and care.

DIY Options: Consider making DIY aromatherapy kits with customized scents and products. This approach allows for greater creativity and ensures that the gifts are unique and meaningful.

Tailored Combinations: Develop combinations of products that complement each other and enhance the recipient's relaxation experience. For example, pair a lavender-scented candle with matching bath salts and essential oils.

Ideas for Creating DIY Aromatherapy Kits
Homemade Blends: Create custom essential oil blends based on the recipient's preferences. Include instructions for use and suggested applications, such as diffuser blends or massage oils.

Packaging and Presentation: Assemble DIY kits in aesthetically pleasing containers, such as glass jars or fabric pouches. Add personal touches, such as handwritten labels or decorative elements, to enhance the presentation.

Themed Kits: Design kits around specific themes, such as sleep aids or stress relief, by including complementary products and scents. This approach ensures that the DIY kit meets the recipient's needs effectively.

Portable Aromatherapy Tools

Aromatherapy Necklaces, Bracelets, and Travel-Friendly Products

Aromatherapy Jewelry: Necklaces and bracelets designed to hold essential oils or diffusing pads provide a portable way to enjoy calming scents throughout the day. These items combine style with functionality.

Travel Diffusers: Compact, travel-sized diffusers are ideal for on-the-go relaxation. They can be used in cars, offices, or hotel rooms to maintain a calming environment wherever the recipient travels.

Essential Oil Roll-Ons: Roll-on bottles with pre-diluted essential oils offer convenience and portability. They are easy to carry and can be applied directly to pulse points for quick stress relief.

How Portable Options Help Manage Anxiety on the Go

Convenience: Portable aromatherapy tools provide easy access to calming scents during busy or stressful moments. They allow individuals to manage anxiety and promote relaxation in various settings.

Consistent Use: Having portable options ensures that relaxation techniques can be integrated into daily routines, enhancing their effectiveness and promoting ongoing stress relief.

Discreet and Functional: Portable tools are designed to be discreet and functional, allowing users to enjoy the benefits of aromatherapy without drawing attention or disrupting their activities.

Gifting Ideas for Men Who Need Relaxation Wherever They Are Travel Kits: Create travel-friendly aromatherapy kits that include essential oils, diffusers, and roll-ons. These kits are perfect for men who frequently travel or have demanding schedules.

Daily Essentials: Consider gifting portable aromatherapy tools that can be easily incorporated into daily routines, such as at the office or during commutes. Practical and stylish options make for thoughtful and useful gifts.

Personalized Items: Personalize portable aromatherapy gifts with the recipient's favorite scents or colors. Customization adds a personal touch and enhances the overall appeal of the gift.

Chapter 5

Fitness and Physical Relaxation Gifts

"Exercise not only changes your body, it changes your mind, your attitude, and your mood."

In today's hectic society, physical activity is more than just a way to stay fit; it's also an effective tool for reducing anxiety and enhancing mental health. In this chapter, we'll look at how exercise and physical relaxation gifts might assist guys with anxiety achieve balance and tranquility. From easy stretching to expert massage tools, these gifts not only promote physical wellness but also help with emotional and mental calm.

The Role of Exercise in Managing Anxiety

The Impact of Regular Physical Activity

Stress Reduction: Regular exercise releases endorphins, which are natural mood lifters that help reduce stress and anxiety.

Improved Mood: Physical activity stimulates the production of serotonin, a neurotransmitter that helps regulate mood and emotional well-being.

Enhanced Sleep Quality: Exercise can improve sleep patterns, leading to better rest and reduced anxiety.

Choosing the Right Type of Exercise

Aerobic Exercise: Activities like jogging, swimming, and cycling increase heart rate and release endorphins, which can significantly reduce anxiety levels.

Strength Training: Building muscle through weight lifting or resistance exercises can also improve mood and help manage stress.

Low-Impact Activities: Gentle exercises such as walking or tai chi can be effective for those who prefer less strenuous options.

Fitness Gear for Physical and Mental Well-being

Comfortable Clothing: Breathable, moisture-wicking exercise wear can enhance comfort and encourage regular physical activity.

Quality Footwear: Properly fitted athletic shoes can prevent injuries and promote a more enjoyable exercise experience.

Fitness Equipment: Consider items like dumbbells, kettlebells, or resistance bands to support varied workout routines.

Gifts for Gentle Movement and Stretching

Resistance Bands

Versatility: Resistance bands can be used for a range of exercises, from stretching to strength training, and are perfect for home workouts.

Portability: Their compact size makes them easy to store and bring along for travel or office use.

Customizable Intensity: Bands come in various resistance levels, allowing users to adjust the intensity of their workouts.

Foam Rollers

Muscle Recovery: Foam rollers help release muscle tension and improve blood flow, which aids in recovery after exercise.

Ease of Use: Simple to use at home, they offer an effective way to relieve sore muscles and promote relaxation.

Variety: Available in different densities and sizes to suit individual needs and preferences.

Yoga Props

Yoga Mats: Provide a comfortable and supportive surface for yoga and stretching exercises.

Blocks and Straps: Help users achieve proper alignment and deepen stretches during yoga practice.

Bolsters: Offer extra support and comfort for restorative yoga poses.

Massage and Relaxation Tools

Massage Guns

Deep Tissue Relief: Massage guns deliver percussive therapy to relieve deep muscle tension and enhance relaxation.

Adjustable Settings: Multiple intensity levels allow for customized massage experiences.

Convenience: Portable and easy to use, making them a great option for home use or on the go.

Heated Massagers
Warmth Therapy: Heat combined with massage helps to relax tight muscles and improve circulation.

Variety of Styles: Options include handheld devices, heated pillows, and massaging pads.

Ease of Use: Many devices come with adjustable heat and massage settings for personalized comfort.

Massage Pillows
Comfortable Relaxation: Designed to provide soothing massages to the neck, shoulders, or back.

Convenient Design: Often include built-in heating functions and easy-to-use controls.

Portable: Can be used at home or in the office for on-the-spot relaxation.

Wearable Fitness Trackers for Mindful Exercise
Monitoring Stress and Activity Levels
Stress Tracking: Some fitness trackers offer stress monitoring features that provide insights into anxiety levels and overall well-being.

Activity Tracking: Measures daily physical activity, sleep patterns, and heart rate to promote a balanced lifestyle.

Goal Setting: Encourages users to set and achieve fitness goals, fostering a sense of accomplishment and reducing stress.

Relaxation-Focused Features
Guided Breathing: Built-in breathing exercises help users practice mindfulness and manage anxiety.

Sleep Analysis: Tracks sleep quality and offers insights for improving rest and relaxation.

Heart Rate Variability: Measures heart rate variability to gauge stress levels and overall health.

Recommendations for Fitness Trackers
Popular Options: Consider well-reviewed models like Fitbit, Garmin, or Apple Watch for their comprehensive features and user-friendly interfaces.

Customization: Look for trackers that offer customizable notifications and features tailored to relaxation and mindfulness.

Compatibility: Ensure the tracker integrates with apps and tools that support stress management and well-being.

Home Fitness Gifts for Relaxation
Creating a Calming Workout Space
Design Considerations: Choose calming colors and decor to create a relaxing exercise environment at home.

Comfortable Flooring: Invest in quality flooring options, such as exercise mats or padded flooring, to enhance comfort during workouts.

Storage Solutions: Organize fitness equipment neatly to maintain a clutter-free and inviting space.

Yoga Mats and Accessories
High-Quality Mats: Opt for mats with good cushioning and grip to support a variety of exercises.

Additional Accessories: Consider adding items like yoga blocks, straps, and bolsters to enhance the workout experience.

Low-Impact Exercise Equipment
Kettlebells: Versatile for strength training and cardiovascular workouts, suitable for home use.

Balance Balls: Great for improving core strength and stability while providing a gentle workout.

Resistance Bands: Ideal for stretching, strengthening, and enhancing flexibility.

Chapter 6

Sleep-Focused Relaxation Gifts

"Sleep is the best meditation." – Dalai Lama

Sleep is a crucial component of mental and physical health, especially for those grappling with anxiety. It's during restful sleep that the body and mind rejuvenate, helping to alleviate stress and promote overall well-being. This chapter explores various sleep-focused relaxation gifts designed to improve sleep quality, ease anxiety, and foster a more restful night's sleep. By focusing on these thoughtful gifts, you can help the men in your life achieve the deep, restorative sleep they need.

The Connection Between Sleep and Anxiety

How Anxiety Affects Sleep and Vice Versa

Disrupted Sleep Patterns: Anxiety often leads to insomnia or frequent awakenings, making it difficult to achieve restorative sleep.

Impact on Mental Health: Poor sleep can exacerbate symptoms of anxiety, creating a vicious cycle of stress and sleeplessness.

Physical Effects: Chronic sleep deprivation contributes to physical health issues such as weakened immune function and increased susceptibility to illness.

The Importance of Sleep for Mental Health
Cognitive Function: Adequate sleep is essential for memory consolidation, decision-making, and emotional regulation.

Stress Management: Quality sleep helps regulate stress hormones, reducing overall anxiety and promoting a more balanced mood.

Physical Recovery: During sleep, the body undergoes vital repair processes that support overall health and resilience.

How Relaxation Gifts Can Improve Sleep Quality
Creating a Sleep-Conducive Environment: Gifts that enhance the sleep environment can significantly improve sleep quality and comfort.

Stress Reduction Tools: Items that promote relaxation before bedtime can help ease the transition into sleep and reduce nighttime anxiety.

Sleep-Inducing Products: Thoughtful gifts designed specifically for better sleep can address common sleep disturbances and support restful nights.

Gifting Weighted Blankets for Deep Sleep
The Science Behind Weighted Blankets and Their Calming Effects
Deep Touch Pressure: Weighted blankets provide gentle, even pressure that can stimulate the production of serotonin and melatonin, promoting relaxation and deeper sleep.

Reduction of Stress Hormones: The calming effect of weighted blankets can lower cortisol levels, which are associated with stress and anxiety.

Improved Sleep Quality: Studies have shown that weighted blankets can improve sleep duration and quality, particularly for individuals with insomnia or anxiety.

Recommendations for the Best Weighted Blankets
Material Choices: Opt for breathable, hypoallergenic fabrics like cotton or bamboo to ensure comfort and reduce overheating.

Weight and Size: Choose a blanket that offers a weight appropriate to the user's body weight (typically 10% of their body weight) and is large enough to cover their body comfortably.

Brand Recommendations: Consider well-reviewed brands such as *Gravity Blankets, YnM, or Layla Sleep* for high-quality options.

How Weighted Blankets Can Become a Staple Relaxation Tool
Consistency: Using a weighted blanket regularly can help establish a calming bedtime routine and enhance overall sleep quality.

Versatility: Weighted blankets can be used during relaxation activities like reading or watching TV, in addition to sleep.

Personalization: Many brands offer customizable options for weight, size, and fabric, allowing you to tailor the gift to the recipient's preferences.

Sleep-Enhancing Tools

Sound Machines

White Noise: Sound machines provide consistent background noise that can mask disruptive sounds and promote a more restful sleep environment.

Nature Sounds: Options like rainfall, ocean waves, or forest sounds can create a soothing atmosphere conducive to relaxation and sleep.

Portability: Many sound machines are compact and travel-friendly, making them useful for creating a calming sleep environment anywhere.

Sleep Masks

Light Blocking: Sleep masks block out light, which can help signal to the brain that it's time to sleep and improve sleep quality.

Comfort and Fit: Look for masks made from soft, breathable materials with adjustable straps for a comfortable and effective fit.

Additional Features: Some masks come with built-in cooling gel or aromatherapy options for added relaxation benefits.

Blackout Curtains

Light Control: Blackout curtains can completely block external light sources, creating a dark and peaceful sleeping environment.

Insulation: They also help insulate the room from temperature fluctuations, contributing to a more consistent and comfortable sleep.

Installation: Choose curtains that are easy to install and fit the size of the windows to ensure optimal effectiveness.

Gifting Combinations for a Complete Sleep Experience
Bundle Ideas: Combine weighted blankets with sound machines and sleep masks for a comprehensive sleep-enhancing gift set.

Personal Touches: Include a note with personalized tips on creating a relaxing bedtime routine to add a thoughtful touch.

Custom Gift Baskets: Create a sleep-themed gift basket with a selection of sleep aids, relaxation products, and comforting treats.

Aromatherapy for Sleep
Essential Oils and Scents for Improving Sleep Quality
Lavender: Known for its calming properties, lavender essential oil is widely used to promote relaxation and improve sleep quality.

Chamomile: Chamomile essential oil helps soothe the nervous system and can aid in falling asleep more easily.

Sandalwood: Sandalwood has a grounding effect that can help quiet the mind and support a restful night's sleep.

How to Use Scents Like Lavender to Encourage Restful Sleep
Diffusers: Use essential oil diffusers to disperse calming scents throughout the bedroom for a relaxing atmosphere.

Pillow Sprays: Lavender pillow sprays can be lightly misted on bedding to create a calming aroma that encourages sleep.

Aromatherapy Roll-Ons: Apply essential oil blends to pulse points before bedtime to enhance relaxation and ease anxiety.

Combining Aromatherapy with Other Sleep-Focused Gifts
Complementary Products: Pair essential oils with weighted blankets, sleep masks, and sound machines to create a multi-faceted relaxation gift set.

Custom Blends: Consider creating personalized essential oil blends that cater to the recipient's specific preferences and needs.

DIY Kits: Provide DIY aromatherapy kits that include essential oils, diffusers, and instructions for creating a calming sleep environment.

Smart Sleep Devices

Sleep Trackers
Monitoring Sleep Patterns: Sleep trackers provide insights into sleep quality, duration, and patterns, helping users identify factors that may affect their rest.

Advanced Features: Some trackers offer additional features like heart rate monitoring, stress level analysis, and personalized sleep recommendations.

Popular Brands: Consider trackers from brands like *Fitbit, Garmin, or Whoop* for comprehensive sleep and health monitoring.

Smart Alarms
Gradual Wake-Up: Smart alarms simulate a natural sunrise with gradual light to wake users gently and improve morning alertness.

Sleep Cycle Analysis: These devices track sleep cycles and wake users during the lightest phase of sleep, leading to a more refreshed feeling upon waking.

Integration: Look for smart alarms that integrate with other wellness apps and devices for a complete sleep management system.

Sleep-Optimized Lighting

Circadian Rhythm Support: Sleep-optimized lighting adjusts color temperature and intensity to align with natural circadian rhythms, supporting better sleep.

Customization: Choose lighting options that offer programmable settings for different times of day and personalized sleep routines.

Gifting Ideas: Consider smart bulbs or lamps with sleep-focused features as part of a holistic sleep improvement gift package.

62

Chapter 7

DIY Relaxation Kits and Personalized Gift Ideas

"The best gifts are the ones that show you truly know the recipient."

Gift-giving is more than just selecting an item; it's about finding something that resonates with the recipient's needs and preferences. For men dealing with anxiety, personalized and thoughtful gifts can provide significant relief and support. This chapter focuses on creating custom relaxation kits, DIY craft gifts, subscription boxes, personalized items, and experience-based gifts—all designed to cater to individual needs and foster a deeper sense of relaxation and well-being.

Creating Custom Relaxation Kits

How to Build Personalized Relaxation Kits for Men with Anxiety

Understanding the Recipient's Needs: Start by identifying what will be most beneficial for the individual. Consider their stress triggers, preferred relaxation methods, and personal preferences.

Selecting the Right Components: Choose items that align with the recipient's needs and interests. For example, if they struggle with sleep, include sleep aids like weighted blankets or calming essential oils. If they enjoy physical activity, consider fitness-related items like resistance bands or massage tools.

Choosing the Right Combination of Products for a Tailored Experience

Balance and Variety: Include a mix of items that address different aspects of relaxation, such as sensory experiences, physical relaxation, and mental well-being. This ensures a well-rounded approach to stress relief.

Quality and Effectiveness: Opt for high-quality products that have proven effectiveness in promoting relaxation and reducing anxiety. This enhances the overall impact of the kit.

Ideas for Themed Kits

Sleep Kit: Include items like a weighted blanket, sleep mask, lavender essential oil, and a white noise machine.

Fitness and Relaxation Kit: Combine resistance bands, a foam roller, a yoga mat, and a fitness tracker.

Mindfulness Kit: Feature a guided meditation app subscription, a mindfulness journal, a set of calming teas, and a stress-relief coloring book.

DIY Craft Gifts for Relaxation

Simple DIY Projects That Promote Relaxation

Homemade Candles: Create candles with soothing scents like lavender or chamomile. Use soy wax or beeswax for a cleaner burn, and add essential oils for an extra touch of relaxation.

Bath Salts: Make bath salts using Epsom salts, sea salt, and essential oils. Customize with scents like eucalyptus or rose to create a calming bath experience.

How to Make Relaxation Crafts That Are Easy and Thoughtful
Step-by-Step Instructions: Provide clear instructions for making each craft, including necessary materials and any special techniques. Include tips on personalization, such as adding a custom label or decorative touch.

Personal Touch: Consider incorporating the recipient's favorite colors, scents, or themes to make the DIY gifts feel more personal and thoughtful.

Personalizing DIY Gifts to Make Them Even More Special
Custom Labels and Packaging: Use personalized labels, tags, or packaging to add a special touch. For example, include a handwritten note with a message of encouragement or well-wishes.

Tailored Scents and Colors: Choose scents and colors that reflect the recipient's preferences or that are known to promote relaxation.

Subscription Boxes for Wellness
Monthly Subscription Boxes That Deliver Relaxation-Focused Products
Regular Deliveries: Subscription boxes provide a steady stream of new and interesting products, offering ongoing support for relaxation and self-care.

Curated Selections: Each box is typically curated with a theme or focus, such as mindfulness, relaxation, or fitness, ensuring that the items are relevant and beneficial.

How These Boxes Provide Continuous Stress Relief and Self-Care
Variety and Discovery: Subscription boxes introduce the recipient to a range of new products and techniques for relaxation, helping them discover what works best for them.

Consistent Encouragement: Regular deliveries serve as a reminder to prioritize self-care and relaxation, reinforcing positive habits.

Recommendations for Wellness and Mindfulness Subscription Services
CalmBox: A subscription box featuring mindfulness and relaxation products, such as calming teas, essential oils, and stress-relief tools.

TheraBox: Offers self-care items and activities aimed at reducing stress and promoting emotional well-being.

Box of Relaxation: Curates products specifically designed for relaxation and stress relief, including bath products, relaxation aids, and comfort items.

Personalized Items for Relaxation
Custom Engraved Tools, Monogrammed Accessories, and Personalized Journals
Engraved Tools: Personalize relaxation tools like massage guns or essential oil diffusers with custom engravings or messages.

Monogrammed Accessories: Include items such as cozy robes or relaxation socks with the recipient's initials for a personal touch.

Personalized Journals: Customize journals with the recipient's name or a motivational quote to encourage mindfulness and reflection.

How Personalization Adds a Meaningful Touch to Relaxation Gifts

Show of Thoughtfulness: Personalized gifts demonstrate that you have put thought into selecting something unique and special for the recipient.

Enhanced Emotional Connection: Customized items can create a stronger emotional connection and make the gift more memorable and appreciated.

Examples of How to Tailor Gifts to the Recipient's Unique Needs
Favorite Colors and Scents: Choose items in the recipient's favorite colors or scents to add a personal touch.

Hobbies and Interests: Consider the recipient's hobbies or interests when selecting or customizing gifts. For example, if they enjoy reading, a personalized book light or reading pillow could be a thoughtful addition.

Experience-Based Gifts for Relaxation

Gifting Experiences Like Spa Days, Massages, or Guided Meditation Sessions
Spa Days: A day at a local spa can provide a complete relaxation experience, including massages, facials, and other treatments designed to alleviate stress.

Massage Sessions: Arrange for a professional massage to target areas of tension and promote relaxation.

Guided Meditation Sessions: Offer a session with a meditation instructor or access to virtual meditation classes to help the recipient learn and practice mindfulness.

How Experiences Create Lasting Memories and Reduce Anxiety
Memorable Moments: Experiences create lasting memories and can have a profound impact on mental well-being, offering a break from daily stressors.

Immediate Benefits: Unlike physical gifts, experiences often provide immediate relaxation and stress relief, contributing to a more positive outlook.

Combining Physical Gifts with Experience-Based Relaxation for a Complete Package
Gift Bundles: Create a comprehensive relaxation package by combining physical gifts, such as relaxation kits or aromatherapy products, with experience-based gifts.

Holistic Approach: A combined approach addresses various aspects of relaxation and stress relief, offering a well-rounded support system for managing anxiety.

Chapter 8

The Art of Gifting: Choosing the Right Relaxation Gifts

"The manner of giving is worth more than the gift." – Pierre Corneille

Presenting a gift is more than just handing over an object; it's about the consideration, attention, and purpose that goes into it. Especially with relaxation gifts, the effect can be deep, offering instant comfort as well as enduring advantages. In this section, we'll explore how to select the perfect gifts for unwinding. We'll consider the preferences of the person you're gifting to, perfect the way you wrap and present your gift, choose the best moment to give it, establish significant traditions, and keep the calm going with thoughtful follow-up presents.

Understanding the Recipient's Needs

How to Assess What Type of Relaxation Gift Will Be Most Beneficial

Evaluate Stress Triggers: Start by understanding what specific aspects of anxiety the recipient is dealing with. Are they struggling with sleep, physical tension, or mental overload?

Identify Preferences: Consider their likes and dislikes. For instance, do they prefer physical relaxation methods like massages, or are they more inclined towards mental practices like meditation?

Questions to Consider When Choosing the Right Gift

1. What are their current stress relief practices? This can help you determine what they might need or appreciate.
2. Are there any specific relaxation tools or techniques they've expressed interest in? This insight can guide you toward a more personalized gift.
3. What is their daily routine like? Understanding their schedule can help you select a gift that seamlessly fits into their lifestyle.

The Importance of Thoughtful Gifting Based on the Recipient's Lifestyle

Tailored to Their Routine: Choose gifts that complement their daily activities. For example, if they have a busy work schedule, a portable relaxation tool like a stress ball or essential oil roll-on might be ideal.

Fit for Their Space: Ensure that the gift is practical for their living situation. For example, if they live in a small apartment, opt for compact items like a travel-sized diffuser instead of a large aromatherapy kit.

The Power of Presentation

How to Present a Gift in a Way That Adds to the Relaxation Experience

Thoughtful Packaging: Use calming colors and textures in your wrapping materials. Soft blues, greens, and earthy tones can enhance the relaxation theme.

Include a Personal Note: A handwritten note with encouraging words can add a personal touch and show that you put thought into the gift.

Tips on Packaging, Wrapping, and Creating an Unboxing Experience

Elegant Wrapping: Choose high-quality wrapping paper or a decorative box that aligns with the relaxation theme. Consider adding elements like ribbon or a simple charm.

Unboxing Experience: Create a serene unboxing experience by arranging the items neatly and adding small touches like dried lavender or a calming quote card.

How Presentation Can Enhance the Emotional Impact of the Gift

Enhance Anticipation: A beautifully presented gift can increase the recipient's excitement and appreciation. The act of unwrapping can itself be a calming and enjoyable experience.

Emotional Connection: Presentation helps convey the thoughtfulness and care behind the gift, making it feel more meaningful and personal.

Timing and Context of Giving

When and How to Give Relaxation Gifts to Maximize Their Impact

Optimal Moments: Consider giving relaxation gifts during times of heightened stress or major life changes, such as after a demanding project or during a stressful period.

Special Occasions: While relaxation gifts are valuable at any time, special occasions like birthdays or anniversaries can be perfect for such thoughtful presents.

Why the Timing of a Gift Can Make a Big Difference in How It's Received

Immediate Relief: Giving a relaxation gift at a time when the recipient is feeling particularly stressed can provide immediate relief and demonstrate your support.

Anticipated Stress: Gifting in anticipation of a stressful event, like a big presentation or family gathering, can be especially appreciated and helpful.

Examples of Situations Where a Relaxation Gift Can Be Especially Meaningful

Post-Illness: A relaxation gift after a period of illness or recovery can support physical and emotional healing.

Work Milestones: Celebrating achievements or promotions with a relaxation gift can help the recipient unwind and enjoy their success.

Creating a Ritual Around Gift-Giving

How to Turn the Act of Giving into a Memorable and Calming Ritual

Establish a Routine: Create a ritual around gift-giving, such as a monthly relaxation-themed evening where the recipient can use their gift and unwind.

Incorporate Relaxation Practices: Combine the gift with a relaxation practice, like setting aside time for a guided meditation session together.

The Benefits of Creating Positive Associations with Relaxation Gifts

Builds Routine: Turning gift-giving into a ritual reinforces the use of relaxation tools and encourages regular practice.

Emotional Benefits: Establishing a positive routine around relaxation can enhance the emotional impact of the gift and provide ongoing comfort.

Ideas for Rituals That Reinforce the Relaxing Nature of the Gift

Weekly Relaxation Time: Encourage the recipient to set aside a specific time each week to use their relaxation gift, such as a Sunday evening bath with bath salts or a Friday night yoga session.

Personalized Rituals: Develop a custom ritual that fits the recipient's preferences, such as incorporating a meditation session with their new mindfulness journal.

Sustaining Relaxation: Follow-Up Gifts

The Importance of Following Up with Additional Gifts or Reminders

Ongoing Support: Regular follow-up gifts or reminders help sustain the recipient's relaxation practices and reinforce the benefits of the initial gift.

Encouragement: A follow-up gift can serve as a motivational boost, reminding the recipient to continue prioritizing their well-being.

How Ongoing Gifting Can Help Reinforce Relaxation Habits

Reinforcing Practice: Gifts that support ongoing relaxation, like a new mindfulness app subscription or a replenished supply of essential oils, help maintain positive habits.

Consistency: Regularly acknowledging the recipient's need for relaxation can encourage consistent self-care and stress management.

Ideas for Small, Thoughtful Follow-Up Gifts to Keep the Relaxation Going

Refill Kits: Provide refills for items like bath salts, essential oils, or stress balls to keep the relaxation routine fresh.

New Additions: Introduce complementary products, such as a new guided meditation album or a relaxation-themed book, to enhance their existing routine.

Choosing presents that aid in relaxation is about truly understanding their needs. It's crucial to present it uniquely, timing it perfectly, and perhaps even turning it into a recurring gesture. Remember to follow up with them to sustain that serene atmosphere. All these efforts demonstrate genuine consideration, not just a perfunctory gesture. It's about positively impacting their day and expressing your concern.

Conclusion

Creating a Lasting Impact Through Thoughtful Gifting

"The best gifts are the ones that keep on giving, long after the box is opened."

At the core of giving gifts is a gesture of love and thoughtfulness. When it comes to choosing relaxation presents for men who deal with anxiety, this gesture becomes even more meaningful. Selecting presents that help ease tension and encourage a calm mind can have positive effects that extend far beyond the excitement of opening them. As we conclude our exploration of relaxation gifts, let's consider the ideas and actions that can have a real and lasting impact.

Recap of Key Points

Understanding the Science of Relaxation Gifts

We've examined how stress affects men both mentally and physically, emphasizing how crucial it is to relax to keep anxiety at bay and prevent burnout.

We've observed how relaxation gifts can engage the mind and senses, demonstrating that the right present can spark joy and help establish habits for long-term relaxation.

Mindfulness and Meditation Gifts

We've discussed tools for mindfulness and meditation, such as apps that guide you through meditation, journals for recording your thoughts, and aids for breathing exercises.

We've noted how activities that involve mindful movement and personalized mindfulness kits can enhance relaxation and foster a sense of peace.

Tech-Free Relaxation Gifts

We've highlighted the importance of taking breaks from our screens and considered non-digital gifts like books, diaries, and nature-inspired items.

We've discovered that getting creative or playing board games can be an excellent way to de-stress and unwind without technology.

Aromatherapy and Scent-Based Relaxation Gifts

We've reviewed how essential oils, fragrant candles, and products with natural scents can make your environment more tranquil.

We've also discussed customizing these scent-based gifts to make them even more special and effective.

Fitness and Physical Relaxation Gifts

The benefits of exercise in managing anxiety and the importance of choosing the right type of physical activity were covered.

We've reviewed gifts for gentle movement, massage tools, wearable fitness trackers, and home fitness equipment that support both physical and mental well-being.

Sleep-Focused Relaxation Gifts
The connection between sleep and anxiety was explored, with a focus on weighted blankets, sleep-enhancing tools, aromatherapy for sleep, and smart sleep devices.

We've highlighted how these gifts can improve sleep quality and contribute to overall mental wellness.

DIY Relaxation Kits and Personalized Gift Ideas
We've discussed how to create custom relaxation kits, DIY craft gifts, and subscription boxes that provide ongoing stress relief.

The importance of personalized items and experience-based gifts was also covered, emphasizing how these can add a meaningful touch to the relaxation journey.

The Art of Gifting: How to Choose the Right Relaxation Gifts
The chapter provided insights into understanding the recipient's needs, presenting gifts thoughtfully, and creating rituals around gift-giving.

We've also explored the significance of follow-up gifts in sustaining relaxation and reinforcing positive habits.

Encouragement to Take Action
So, when you're thinking about the men in your life who could benefit from some stress relief, remember that giving a thoughtful gift is more than just presenting something nice. It's about selecting items that truly meet their needs and preferences, and offering them in a way that

demonstrates your care. By choosing gifts that target specific stressors and promote relaxation, you're not just giving an object—you're facilitating better mental health and a more balanced life.

Keep in mind the key points we've discussed in this guide as you make your gift selections. Whether it's tools for staying present, items that don't require a power button, or gifts that feel personal, strive to create an experience that resonates with the recipient and supports their pursuit of peace and balance.

Final Thoughts on the Power of Thoughtful Gifting

Final Thoughts on the Impact of Caring Gifts

Giving from the heart can have a profound impact. It's a way of showing you understand and care, and it can bring comfort, relief, and happiness long after the gift has been given. By focusing on gifts that assist with anxiety and enhance well-being, you're contributing to a calmer and more enjoyable life for those you love.

Ultimately, the best presents are those that continue to give, nurturing mental health and improving life. When you give with purpose and consideration, you're not just handing over a gift—you're offering a lasting treasure of tranquility and relaxation.

Review

We Value Your Feedback!

Thank you for choosing *Relaxation Gifts for Men with Anxiety: Thoughtful Ideas to Calm the Mind, Soothe the Soul, and Reclaim Serenity*. Your support means the world to me, and I hope the book has provided you with valuable insights and practical ideas to help those you care about.

Share Your Experience

If you enjoyed the book, I would be incredibly grateful if you could take a few moments to leave a review. Your feedback helps other readers find the book and allows me to continue creating content that supports mental well-being.

To leave a review, please visit my [Author Central Page](https://www.amazon.com/author/your-author-central-link) where you can share your thoughts and rate the book. Your honest review can make a significant difference!

www.ingramcontent.com/pod-product-compliance
Lightning Source LLC
Chambersburg PA
CBHW061516250726
48657CB00005B/1895